Companion to the Lectionary
2. Hymns and Anthems

Alan Dunstan and Martin Ellis

Companion to the Lectionary

2. Hymns and Anthems

EPWORTH PRESS

First published 1983
by Epworth Press

Enquiries should be addressed to
Epworth Press, Room 195,
1 Central Buildings,
Westminster,
London SW1H 9NR

7162 0373 1

Phototypeset by Input Typesetting Ltd
and printed in Great Britain by
The Camelot Press Ltd
Southampton

Contents

Note for the Reader

John Stacey

Chairman, Editorial Committee, Epworth Press

This book has, in addition to this Note, a Foreword and four Prefaces. The reasons for this extravagance are that it was judged that comments upon the selection of hymns and anthems would best be made by those who had selected them and that in an Anglican-Methodist enterprise a Foreword from an ecumenical liturgist would be an advantage.

Not every user of this book will necessarily be seeking to construct a service based directly upon the Lectionary. At the same time, the themes for the Sundays are important to universal Christian teaching. For this reason there are two entrances upon the body of the book. Those using the book in conjunction with the Lectionary should consult Subject Index 1, whereas those wishing to use the material from a thematic point of view should consult Subject Index 2.

Foreword

A. Raymond George

The Church has always allowed great freedom in the choice of hymns and anthems. In the Church of England *The Book of Common Prayer*, which prescribes forms of service in considerable detail, including the passages of scripture to be read, makes no attempt to lay down rules to govern the choice of hymns and anthems, apart from the hymn in the Ordination Service, and the various alternative services of recent years leave a similar freedom. Methodism authorizes an official service book, but its forms are not intended 'to curb creative freedom, but rather to provide norms for its guidance'. But no such norms are provided for hymns and anthems. Yet hymns play a more significant part in the worship of Methodism and the other Free Churches than they do in the Church of England; indeed they have been described as 'the Dissenting Use'.

In recent years, however, a new factor has entered the situation, namely the use of a common lectionary. In 1967 the Joint Liturgical Group published *Calendar and Lectionary* (ed. R. C. D. Jasper), and probably all the Churches in England and Scotland (except the Roman Catholic) which use a lectionary at all are now using it in some form, with certain small adaptations jointly made by some churches. The Church of England has, with some further adaptations, included it in the *Alternative Service Book 1980* as the Lectionary for the Eucharist. *The Methodist Service Book* (1975) follows it almost exactly, except for the Special Days. (The earlier days of Holy Week, which are not mentioned in *The Methodist Service Book*, have been added here.) Methodists, though free in this as in other aspects of worship, are increasingly using this lectionary. The time thus seems ripe to consider what hymns and anthems are appropriate to it. The list published here is of course entirely unofficial; everyone is free to use it or not. A wise use of freedom, however, involves the consideration of expert guidance, and many leaders of worship and choirmasters will be glad of the suggestions made here by experienced ministers and musicians.

The suggestions are intended for the morning service, whether or not that is or includes Holy Communion. The lectionary is on a two-year cycle; the first year begins on the ninth Sunday before Christmas in 1984, 1986, and so on.

I hope these suggestions will be widely used.

The Choice of Hymns from *The Methodist Hymn Book*

Wilfrid J. Little

The procedure has been to make notes of the set passages of scripture, view them in the light of the collect and title for the day, and then turn to the hymn books.

Fortunately, all the major Methodist books from Wesley's *Collection of Psalms and Hymns*, Charlestown 1737, onwards, were available. *Partners in Learning* also has been carefully noted and the contemporary Christian concerns for the preservation of the earth, the true human freedoms, ecumenism and the purifying of society, have been kept constantly in mind.

Since in many churches the Junior Church or Sunday School stays with the adult congregation for the second hymn, a hymn suitable for young people has been included.

The Choice of Hymns from *Hymns & Psalms*
Kenneth Trickett

The committee responsible for the compilation of *Hymns & Psalms* constantly had in mind the requirements of a book which could adequately take its place alongside the lectionary, and the sectional arrangement of the contents, together with comprehensive indexes, will be found to facilitate the choice of hymns appropriate to specific themes. In making my selection I have had regard to hymns intended specially for certain Sundays or festivals of the Christian year; hymns based on or containing references to the set themes and passages of scripture; hymns suitable for young people; hymns appropriate only when the Lord's Supper is being observed, but nevertheless relevant in other respects. I have aimed at a variety of metres and styles in each set of hymns, though it will often be advisable not to confine one's choice to those suggested, but rather to include other hymns so as to ensure a balanced order of worship.

The Choice of Hymns from the Anglican Tradition

Alan Dunstan

The *Alternative Service Book* has provided us with the lessons that ought to be read, but this book is by no means intended to direct the hymns that ought to be sung. Many of the hymns suggested in these lists will not be wanted at all by those who consult them. Some will be beyond the competence of particular choirs and organists, others will not be suitable for certain congregations, and others will be outside the preferences of those who choose the hymns.

These considerations will be obvious to the reader. But there is another point that is not so obvious to those who consult these lists. Although we have three lessons for each Sunday, linked by a general theme, that theme is *so* general that the widest variations may be played upon it. When the Liturgical Group's *Calendar and Lectionary*, OUP 1967, it stated in its own Report (*The Calendar and Lessons*, SPCK 1968): 'The thematic titles provided are no more than indications of emphasis. They are not intended to dictate to the biblical material, and should not be allowed to do so.'

In the *Alternative Service Book*, the Sunday themes are not printed with the readings but on a separate page (1092). We are told (p. 981 n.2) that when two lessons are read, the Gospel must always be one of them, and an asterisk indicates which of the other two is to be preferred in such cases. This is the only recognition of the principle of a 'controlling lesson', first envisaged by the Joint Liturgical Group, and again the asterisk is not printed with the readings but in Table 3a (pp. 1049ff.).

In the course of the Anglican revision of the lectionary, the idea of general themes has therefore been played down – perhaps in order that preachers and others responsible for the service shall not miss the richness and variety latent in the biblical material for each Sunday. This is the second reason why the lists of hymns provided here can be no more than a guide. And this must mean that the choice of hymns (as well as other variable parts of the liturgy) ought to be a fresh and creative exercise each year.

This was the main thesis of my book *These are the Hymns*, SPCK 1973, but I have spelt it out again with specific reference to the *Alternative Service Book* in *The Hymn Explosion*, RSCM 1981, esp. pp. 17–19. However, it may be helpful to give another practical illustration of what I mean. Look at Pentecost 10 – Year 2. The general theme is 'The Mind of Christ', and the appointed lessons are I Samuel 24.9–17; Galatians 6.1–10; Luke 7.36–50. These passages suggest a multiplicity of themes to the preacher. He might examine the character of Saul, or look at the contrast between Gal. 6.2 and Gal 6.5; from Gal. 6.7–10 he might take the theme of perseverance; and if he turned to the Gospel, the story itself and the various parts of it suggest a variety of approaches. No standard list could cover all these possibilities for Pentecost 10 in Year 2. If Gal. 6.7–10 were the theme, the hymns, using *Ancient & Modern Revised* and *One Hundred Hymns for Today*, might be:

Introit: 412; Gradual: T41; Offertory: 292; Post Communion: T83

But if it were Luke 7.47, the choice (from the same books) might be:

Introit: 187; Gradual: T41; Offertory: 195; Post Communion: T 70

Only the Gradual hymn would be common to both lists. This is not to suggest that the sermon should invariably dictate the choice of all the hymns; those selected in these lists will be seen to be suitable for the parts of the service for which they are intended, but at the same time they reflect the theme that has been chosen for this particular eucharist.

Since the publication of the *Alternative Service Book*, two books have offered help in the choice of hymns for services. *A Hymn Guide* – compiled by a group in the York Diocese – has suggested hymns appropriate to the general Sunday themes from a variety of hymn books commonly used in the Church of England. After some of the hymns, the figures 1 and 2 denote the year for which the hymn is more appropriate. In *Hymns with the New Lectionary*, Robin Leaver has ranged more widely and ecumenically in his choice of hymn books and the left-hand margin suggests the scriptural passage to which the suggested hymn relates.

The aim of this work is at once more modest and more precise. It is more modest in that it is confined to books most widely found in our Church; thus one list is based upon *Ancient & Modern Revised* and its two supplements, *One Hundred Hymns for Today* (indicated by T) and *More Hymns for Today* (indicated by M). The second list is based upon the *English Hymnal* and its supplement *English Praise* (indicated by the letter P). Cross reference will obviously be necessary if the *English Hymnal*, for example, is used in conjunction with one of the supplements to *Hymns Ancient & Modern*.

But the aim of this work is also more precise. It is concerned with choosing hymns specifically for the Eucharist. In each case four hymns are provided. They are:

1. The Introit: the opening act of worship and gathering together of the congregation.
2. The Gradual: designed to link the epistle and gospel, and therefore probably unsuitable if the epistle is omitted.
3. The Offertory: intended to be suitable both to that point in the service, and also to the general theme selected for the day (it is likely, therefore, to be the most variable of the four).
4. The Post-Communion hymn designed in Rite A and Rite B to be sung before the Blessing and Dismissal so that the strength of neither is weakened.

I have not made provision for processions, since customs vary so much from place to place, or for hymns to be sung during the administration, as these are much less directly related to the themes and readings than are the other hymns. I have tried to observe the normal conventions about the length of hymns (e.g. short for Gradual, long for Offertory) where possible, but I cannot regard this as an over-riding consideration where a choice has to be made. The lists try to ensure a certain variety – of style, metre and mood – in any particular service, and to indicate how, by careful planning, repetition may be avoided and hymns spread over a two-year period. The omission of some well-known hymns implies no judgment upon them, but simply that they are not immediately suggested by the themes or the readings for the day.

The Preface to the Musical Material in *Hymns & Anthems*

Martin Ellis

In the Introduction to *The Guide to the Use of the Revised Edition of Hymns Ancient & Modern*, the writer says:

> The lists do not provide schemes to suit the needs of every type of church or service, since that would manifestly be impossible. They are rather suggestions, drawn up with the average parish church in mind, which can be used frequently as they stand, but perhaps more often as a preliminary framework. Within this framework certain hymns will remain as suitable, while others will be replaced by those which are considered more appropriate for use on a particular occasion. The lists will not, however, be rightly used if regarded as a time-and-trouble saver, to be copied automatically, week by week, year after year. Hardly a Sunday ought to pass without the inclusion of one hymn or more which is not suggested in these lists, for no one but the parish priest himself can rightly judge the devotional needs of his flock.

The same can be said of the musical material suggested in the lists which follow in this book. It must be made clear that we are dealing with the themes found in the Lectionaries of the Anglican and Methodist Churches in Great Britain associated with the *Alternative Service Book 1980* and the Methodist Service Book. Those who seek guidance for the use of hymns in the Prayer Book Services (1662) and the Book of Offices (1936) will find it in *The Guide to the Use of the Revised Edition of Hymns Ancient & Modern* (Clowes), *Subject, Textual and Lineal Indexes to the Methodist Hymn Book*, and at the end of *The English Hymnal* (1933). It is clear now that uniformity is not the desired aim of the contributors to this section of the book.

The Rev. Canon Alan Dunstan, Precentor of Gloucester Cathedral, sometime Vice-Principal of Ripon College, Cuddesdon, and author of *These are the Hymns*, together with the Rev. Wilfrid Little, Methodist Minister, Vice-Chairman of the

Hymn Society of Great Britain and Ireland and a founder member of the Methodist Church Music Society, and Mr Kenneth Trickett, sometime executive member of each of these Societies and author of reviews and articles in the field of hymnology, represent the evangelical zeal of the two Societies and desire above all else to set a good example in the method of choosing hymns for our time of worship together. It will be noticed that in some cases the choice of hymns is limited to *Hymns & Psalms* (1983), *The Methodist Hymn Book* (1933) and *Hymns & Songs* (1969) in the section called 'Festivals and Special Occasions'. Some of the 'Special Occasions' are not observed normally in Anglican worship; and arrangements for Holy Week, Good Friday and the Easter Vigil vary a good deal according to local custom.

It is hoped that the person in the pew may be given greater opportunities in preparing for Sunday worship. Clergy and those members of the laity who are in charge of the music are urged to set aside some part of the week previous to any given Sunday or Festival Day in the proper practice of the tunes to the hymns and the teaching in the doctrinal content of the texts to the end that our people may 'sing praise with understanding'.

At the request of the Executive of the Methodist Church Music Society within the Division of Ministries of the Methodist Church of Great Britain, I have drawn up a list of anthems. On closer examination it can be seen that the emphasis is laid upon the suitable contents of available collections. For the sake of economy the purchase of music in this form is recommended to churches embarking on the formation of a choir or replenishment of the choir library. Although the anthems suggested are classified under grades of technical difficulty, most competent choirs will use a balanced repertoire from Lists A, B & C. This is to be expected in the light of wise forward planning by a good choir trainer. List A is generally simple. Some members are for unison voices and others for two- or three-part singing. List B is dealt with in greater detail than lists A or C, containing music often described as 'the bread and butter repertoire'. List C is intended for choirs with competent solo voices and a good choral technique. Some numbers are settings of Latin texts which even now remain debatable in their use within Free Church Worship.

The compilers of this section strive to encourage the adoption of the highest possible standards of care and attention in this musical area of our worship. We urge clergy and choir leaders alike to use music to enhance our church services and not to cause a form of spiritual indigestion amongst the congregations in their charge.

Subject Index 1

Days to Subjects

A = Anglican; M = Methodist; (i) = First Year; (ii) = Second Year

Subject Index 1

Subject Index 2

Subjects to Days

a = after; b = before; C = Christmas; Ep = Epiphany;
E = Easter; P = Pentecost; (i) = First Year; (ii) = Second Year

Days (Anglican)	Subject	Days (Methodist)
1. 7bE	Christ, the Friend of Sinners	–
2. 8bE	Christ, the Healer	8bE
3. 9bE	Christ, the Teacher	9bE
4. –	Christ, the Worker of Miracles	7bE
5. P23	Citizens of Heaven	aP20
6. P20	Endurance	aP21
7. 5aE	Going to the Father	5aE
8. –	Life for the World	EpIV(ii)
9. EpVI	Parables	–
10. EpIII	Signs of Glory	–
11. 4bC	The Advent Hope	4bC
12. 1bC	The Annunciation	1bC
13. 6aE	The Ascension of Christ	6aE
14. EpI	The Baptism of Christ/Jesus	EpI
15. 1aE(ii)	The Bread of Life	1aE(ii)
16. 4aE(i)	The Charge to Peter	4aE(i)
17. P21	The Christian Hope	–
18. P3(ii)	The Church's Confidence in Christ	aP3(ii)
19. P4(ii)	The Church's Mission to the Individual	aP4(ii)
20. P5(ii)	The Church's Mission to All Men	aP5(ii)
21. P2(ii)	The Church's Unity and Fellowship	aP2(ii)
22. 9bC	The Creation	9bC
23. 7bC	The Election of God's People: Abraham	7bC

Days (Anglican)	Subject	Days (Methodist)
24. 2aE(i)	The Emmaus Road	2aE(i)
25. 8bC	The Fall	8bC
26. P14	The Family	aP15
27. 2bC	The Forerunner	2bC
28. EpII	The First Disciples	EpII
29. P4(i)	The Freedom of the Sons of God	P4:1
30. –	The Friend of Sinners	EpIV(i)
31. P8	The Fruit of the Spirit	aP8
32. 2aE(ii)	The Good Shepherd	2aE(ii)
33. 2aC	The Holy Family	–
34. –	The Holy Mountain	EpVI(ii)/aP22(i)
35. 1aC	The Incarnation	–
36. 5bE	The King and the Kingdom: Conflict	5bE
37. 4bE	The King and the Kingdom: Suffering	4bE
38. 6bE	The King and the Kingdom: Temptation	6bE
39. 3bE	The King and the Kingdom: Transfiguration	3bE
40. 2bE	The King and the Kingdom: The Victory of the Cross	2bE
41. 3aE(i)	The Lakeside	3aE(i)
42. P19	The Life of Faith	aP19
43. P3(i)	The Life of the Baptized	aP3(i)
44. P10	The Mind of Christ	aP10
45. P7	The More Excellent Way	aP7
46. P16	The Neighbour	aP14
47. –	The New Dispensation	EpV(i)/P23(ii)
48. P5(i)	The New Law	aP5(i)
49. P6	The New Man	aP6
50. EpIV	The New Temple	EpIII(ii)
51. P18	The Offering of Life	aP18
52. P2(i)	The People of God	aP2(i)
53. –	The Presentation in the Temple	2aC(i)

Subject Index 2

Hymn Book Abbreviations

AMR   *Ancient & Modern Revised*
           T   : *One Hundred Hymns for Today*
           M : *More Hymns for Today*
EH   *English Hymnal*
           P   : *English Praise*
HP   *Hymns – Psalms* (1983)
MHB   *Methodist Hymn Book* (1933)
           HS : *Hymns and Songs* (1969)

NB: (i) and (ii) after hymn book abbreviations refer to the year of the lectionary cycle.

Set 1, Set 2 etc. refer to the choices where more than one set of readings is given in the *Alternative Service Book*. Set 1 implies that the first OT lesson, NT lesson and Gospel will be chosen, Set 2 the second, and so on.

Hymns and Anthems

1.   Christ, the Friend of Sinners

Hymns	HP	(i) 136 : 146 : 217 : 235 : 713
		(ii) 219 : 257 : 559 : 729 : 767
	AMR	(i) 185 : T29 : T50 : 367
		or (M178) (M180)
		(ii) 365 : 189 pt 2 : T55 : 186
	EH	(i) 471 : P24 : 414 : 424
		(ii) 470 : 419 pt 2 : 316 : 390
Anthems	A	30 : 31
	B	(i) 8
		(ii) 31
	C	76 : 85

2. Christ, the Healer

Hymns	MHB	(i) 314 : 847 : 51HS : 236 : 794
		(ii) 7 : 847 : 39HS : 236 : 155
	HP	(i) 140 : 152 : 398 : 744 : 766
		(ii) 29 : 148 : 391 : 395 : 396
	AMR	(i) 208 : 210 : T2 : 196
		(ii) T73 : 193 : 478 : 266
	EH	(i) 408 : 477 : 349 : 446
		(ii) 258 : 414 : 526 : 553
Anthems	A	3 : 89
	B	(i) 127
		(ii) 61
	C	24

3. Christ, the Teacher

Hymns	MHB	(i) 91 : 868 : 549 : 73HS : 600
		(ii) 161 : 34HS : 549 : 599 : 598
	HP	(i) 133 : 134 : 211 : 313 : 734
		(ii) 137 : 232 : 540 : 737 : 802
	AMR	(i) 7 : 473 : T59 : T13 (or M 125)
		(ii) 223 : T84 : T77 : 331 om. v. 2
		or M113 M105
	EH	(i) 434 : 167 : P58 : P101
		(ii) 512 vv. 1, 6, 7, 8 : P70 : P65 : 577 om.
		v. 2

Anthems	A	59 : 80
	B	(i) 55
		(ii) 83
	C	51 : 99

4. Christ, the Worker of Miracles

Hymns	MHB	(i) 924 : 167 : 155 : 561 : 309
		(ii) 91 : 167 : 509 : 919 : 432
	HP	(i) 144 : 150 : 215 : 390 : 457
		(ii) 65 : 153 : 264 : 423 : 693
Anthems	A	51 : 25
	B	(i) 112
		(ii) 88
	C	71 : 77

5. Citizens of Heaven

Hymns	MHB	(i) 363 : 855 : 37HS : 831 : 320
		(ii) 668 : 244 : 818 : 428 : 652B

| | HP | (i) 439 : 485 : 679 : 818 : 821 |
| | | (ii) 209 : 484 : 815 : 817 : 819 |

      HP   (i) 439 : 485 : 679 : 818 : 821
               (ii) 209 : 484 : 815 : 817 : 819

      AMR (i) 272 : 258 : 281 : 639
               (ii) 283 : 278 : 286 : 298

      EH   (i) 428 : 375 : 465 : 624
               (ii) P41 : 412 : P82 : 425

Anthems A   36 : 77

      B   (i) 66
            (ii) 20 : 49

      C   18 : 78 : 117 : 27

6. Endurance

Hymns   MHB (i) 71 : 894 : 158 : 489 : 246
               (ii) 415 : 620 : 340 : 636 : 705

      HP   (i) 378 : 661 : 670 : 686 : 716
               (ii) 233 : 667 : 675 : 682 : 689

      AMR (i) 299 : 209 : T10 : 292
               (ii) 165 : 304 : 296 : 417

      EH   (i) 447 : 402 : P75 : 503
               (ii) 450 : 389 : 397 : 310

Anthems A   65 : 80

      B   (i) 107
            (ii) 93

      C   111 : 39

7. Going to the Father

Hymns   MHB (i) 73 : 53 : 229 : 544 : 85
               (ii) 932 : 856 : 454 : 708 : 271

| | HP | (i) 243 : 401 : 433 : 557 : 813 |
| | | (ii) 203 : 255 : 458 : 558 : 751 |

HP   (i) 243 : 401 : 433 : 557 : 813
       (ii) 203 : 255 : 458 : 558 : 751

AMR (i) 222 : T69 : 606 vv. 1–5 : 605
       or   M168
       (ii) 142 : 209 : 318 : 421

EH   (i) 380 : P33 : 565 vv. 1–5 : P30
       (ii) P41 : 627 : 474 : P105

Anthems A   36 : 52

          B   (i) 125
                  (ii) 104

          C   59 : 73

8. Life for the World

Hymns   MHB 114 : 8HS : 93 : 49 : 318

          HP   226 : 261 : 290 : 321 : 725

Anthems A   94

          B   16 : 21 : 65

          C   48

9. Parables

Hymns   HP   249 : 466 : 482 : 628 : 768

          AMR 309 : 251 : T96 : 327
          or   M116 M115 M 135

          EH   P60 : 449 : P72 : 436

Anthems A   88

          B   124

          C   31 : 91

10. Signs of Glory

Hymns	HP	(i)	4 : 168 : 242 : 253 : 818
		(ii)	78 : 457 : 459 : 616 : 633
	AMR	(i)	376 : T9 : 81 : 209
		(ii)	T4 : 301 : 413 : 257
	EH	(i)	P88 : P69 : 47 : 425
		(ii)	165 : P74 : 321 : 393
Anthems	A		32 : 69
	B	(i)	75
		(ii)	112
	C		55 : 106

11. The Advent Hope

Hymns	MHB	(i)	257 : 82 : 255 : 253 : 264
		(ii)	257 : 82 : 254 : 261 : 264
	HP	(i)	82 : 85 : 245 : 249 : 449
		(ii)	85 : 241 : 425 : 448 : 670
	AMR	(i)	49 : T9 : 47 : 51
		(ii)	45 : 47 : 55 : T97
		or M150	
	EH	(i)	8 : P4 : 5 : 7
		(ii)	1 : 5 : 12 : P99
Anthems	A		8 : 26
	B	(i)	12 : 94 : 116
		(ii)	12 : 47 : 94
	C		32 : 33 : 113 : 39

12. The Annunciation

Hymns	MHB	(i) 60HS : 857 : 64HS : 83 : 950
		(ii) 64HS : 60 HS : 950 : 83 : 805
	HP	(i) 79 : 87 : 108 : 240 : 512
		(ii) 77 : 81 : 83 : 86 : 724
	AMR	(i) 54 : 335 : T89 : 53
		(ii) 49 : T76 : 363 : 51
		or M151
	EH	(i) P1 : 370 : P49 : 6
		(ii) 8 : P4 : 585 : 7
Anthems	A	5 : 21
	B	(i) 80
		(ii) 51
	C	17 : 32 : 33

13. The Ascension of Christ

Hymns	MHB	(i) 221 : 224 : 222 : 226 : 228
		(ii) 221 : 225 : 230 : 226 : 231
	HP	(i) 189 : 190 : 209 : 253 : 616
		(ii) 201 : 210 : 222 : 271 : 810
	AMR	(i) 216 : 148 om. v. 4 : 399 : 610 vv. 7–9
		(ii) 150 : 147 vv. 3–6 : 400 : 218
	EH	(i) 476 : 145 pt 1 : 301 : 143 vv. 7–9
		(ii) 148 : 143 vv. 3–6 : 319 : 147
Anthems	A	26 : 27
	B	(i) 84
		(ii) 37
	C	5 : 15 : 23 : 41 : 62 : 113

14. The Baptism of Christ/Jesus

Hymns	MHB	(i)	62 : 400 : 99 : 817 : 730
		(ii)	62 : 416 : 2HS : 17HS : 632
	HP	(i)	84 : 129 : 132 : 303 : 732
		(ii)	125 : 229 : 313 : 322 : 773
	AMR	(i)	80 : 192 : T87 : 459
		or	M107 M109
		(ii)	81 : 260 : 187 : T45
	EH	(i)	43 : 405 : P23 : 341
		(ii)	47 : P23 : 459 : 598
Anthems	A		18 : 54
	B	(i)	105
		(ii)	129
	C		69

15. The Bread of Life

Hymns	MHB	217 : 95 : 55HS : 509 : 13HS
	HP	137 : 467 : 599 : 697 : 730
	AMR	128 : T69 : 129 : 135
	EH	139 : P33 : 125 : 625
Anthems	A	22 : 41
	B	17 : 34
	C	77

16. The Charge to Peter

Hymns	MHB	356 : 703 : 348 : 791 : 435
	HP	50 : 499 : 521 : 772 : 809

	AMR or	131 : 355 : 554 : 136 M104
	EH	P38 : 578 : 227 : 129
Anthems	A	67
	B	121
	C	23

17. The Christian Hope

Hymns	HP	(i) 63 : 416 : 552 : 571 : 672 (ii) 425 : 669 : 678 : 680 : 749
	AMR	(i) 314 : T64 : T56 : T3 or M130 (ii) 377 : 178 : T14 : T3
	EH	(i) 367 : 409 : 381 : P73 or P64 (ii) 532 : 93 : 371 : P73
Anthems	A	49 : 74
	B	(i) 74 (ii) 24
	C	9 : 41

18. The Church's Confidence in Christ

Hymns	MHB	72 : 249 : 697 : 316 : 246
	HP	2 : 80 : 258 : 681 : 811
	AMR or	243 : 190 : 387 : T45 M107
	EH	P56 : 506 : 418 : 598
Anthems	A	51
	B	49
	C	9 : 56

19. The Church's Mission to the Individual

Hymns	MHB	417 : 840 : 540 : 416 : 284
	HP	136 : 457 : 620 : 744 : 794
	AMR or	7 : 102 vv.1, 2, 7 : 351 : T62 M192
	EH	258 : P27 vv.1, 2, 7 : 574 : P74
Anthems	A	47
	B	58
	C	75

20. The Church's Mission to All Men

Hymns	MHB	1 : 864 : 75 : 40HS : 272
	HP	520 : 774 : 775 : 782 : 807
	AMR	264 : T43 : 220 : 306
	EH	395 : P95 : 420 : 549
Anthems	A	62
	B	45 : 66
	C	7 : 99

21. The Church's Unity and Fellowship

Hymns	MHB	659 : 701 : 717 : 35HS : 714
	HP	495 : 547 : 754 : 779 : 806
	AMR	43 : T47 : 403 : 292
	EH	P57 : P97 : P64 : 503 pt 1
Anthems	A	12
	B	77
	C	72

22. The Creation

Hymns	MHB	(i)	46 : 851 : 56HS : 20 : 10HS
		(ii)	495 : 547 : 754 : 779 : 806
	HP	(i)	16 : 24 : 29 : 330 : 335
		(ii)	7 : 260 : 333 : 334 : 339
	AMR	(i)	167 : 225 vv. 1–4 : 246 : 368
	or		M165
		(ii)	174 : 160 : T78 or M160 : T83
	EH	(i)	466 : 368 vv. 1–3 : P91 : 535 pt 1
		(ii)	P93 : 162 : P87 : P77
Anthems	A		12 : 38
	B	(i)	6 : 97
		(ii)	97 : 107
	C		57 : 93

23. The Election of God's People: Abraham

Hymns	MHB	(i)	34 : 630 : 21A : 362 : 272
		(ii)	21A : 630 : 607 : 362 : 116
	HP	(i)	239 : 437 : 447 : 675 : 693
		(ii)	378 : 442 : 452 : 453 : 662
	AMR	(i)	T94 : T39 : 631 vv. 1, 8–10 : 296
		(ii)	374 : 631 vv. 1–5 : 255 : 310
	EH	(i)	P57 : 439 : 646 vv. 1, 4–8 : 397
		(ii)	P90 : 646 vv.1–4 : 489 : 480
Anthems	A		49 : 83
	B	(i)	35
		(ii)	1
	C		41 : 107

24. The Emmaus Road

Hymns	MHB	684 : 208 : 307 : 16HS : 247
	HP	52 : 199 : 605 : 610 : 645
	AMR or	128 : 129 : T16 : 602 vv. 11–13 M144
	EH	139 : 125 vv. 1–4 : P61 : P37
Anthems	A	82
	B	69
	C	36

25. The Fall

Hymns	MHB	(i) 38 : 242 : 15HS : 1 : 560 (ii) 924 : 922 : 173 : 1 : 686
	HP	(i) 245 : 412 : 419 : 420 : 429 (ii) 185 : 231 : 405 : 427 : 430
	AMR	(i) 169 : 236 : 164 : 297 (ii) 185 : 325 : T36 : 411
	EH	(i) 441 : P76 : P99 : 304 (ii) 471 : 82 : 387 : 304
Anthems	A	7 : 87
	B	(i) 9 (ii) 29
	C	34 : 71

26. The Family

Hymns	MHB	(i) 12 : 865 : 59HS : 717 : 781 (ii) 172 : 798 : 59HS : 59 : 781

| | HP | (i) 333 : 366 : 369 : 374 : 495 |
| | | (ii) 367 : 368 : 371 : 636 : 762 |

	AMR	(i) 4 : 632 : T74 : 373
	or	M172
		(ii) 171 : T68 : 274 : 450
	or	M161

| | EH | (i) 260 : P47 : 529 : 535 pt 2 |
| | | (ii) 519 : 396 : 309 vv. 1–5 : 401 |

Anthems A 38 : 31

B (i) 32
   (ii) 82

C 19 : 60 : 61

27. The Forerunner

Hymns MHB (i) 115 : 57HS : 778 : 581 : 603
          (ii) 57HS : 585 : 584 : 301 : 783

      HP (i) 84 : 245 : 449 : 456 : 457
          (ii) 84 : 236 : 241 : 248 : 249

      AMR (i) 50 : 229 : T51 : 263
          (ii) 52 : 216 : 50 : 54

      EH (i)   9 : 518 : P50 : 504
          (ii) 492 : 476 :   9 : P1

Anthems A 29 : 46

B (i) 65 : 130
   (ii) 65 : 11

C 48 : 102

28. The First Disciples

Hymns MHB (i) 69HS : 858 : 98HS : 509   : 780
          (ii) 33   : 157 : 69HS : 98HS : 603

HP	(i) 139 : 153 : 211 : 673 : 705
	(ii) 141 : 523 : 535 : 704 : 745
AMR	(i) T12 : 541 : 184 : 328
	(ii) 226 : 542 : 533 : T49
or	M183
EH	(i) P89 : 207 : 383 : 344
	(ii) P94 : P78 : 205 : 417

Anthems

A	4 : 28
B	(i) 22 : 47
	(ii) 23 : 47
C	54

29. The Freedom of the Sons of God

Hymns

MHB	42HS : 394 : 568 : 546 : 447
HP	607 : 656 : 666 : 714 : 774
AMR	8 : T58 : 259 : T25
EH	165 : 303 : 464 : 415

Anthems

A	76
B	24
C	65

30. The Friend of Sinners

Hymns

MHB	100 : 841 : 154 : 94HS : 369
HP	9 : 149 : 460 : 729 : 805

Anthems

A	31
B	8
C	66 : 76

31. The Fruit of the Spirit

Hymns	MHB	(i) 11 : 864 : 291 : 537 : 74HS
		(ii) 363 : 279 : 527 : 605 : 589
	HP	(i) 284 : 289 : 313 : 320 : 461
		(ii) 314 : 318 : 321 : 326 : 492
	AMR	(i) 2 : 230 : 406 : T26
		M182 : M130 M170
		(ii) 239 : 532 : T20 : 418
		or M106
	EH	(i) 52 vv.1–3, 9 : 157 : P42 : P67
		(ii) P72 : 454 : 384 : 315
Anthems	A	45 : 53
	B	(i) 79
		(ii) 25
	C	108

32. The Good Shepherd

Hymns	MHB	621 : 76 : 318 : 457 : 791
	HP	69 : 230 : 263 : 750 : 772
	AMR	131 : 197 : 415 : 140
	or	M110
	EH	P32 : 490 : 602 : 134
Anthems	A	68 : 83
	B	93
	C	95

33. The Holy Family

| Hymns | HP | (i) 146 : 152 : 154 : 173 : 367 |
| | | (ii) 99 : 114 : 143 : 266 : 383 |

	AMR	(i) M166 : 78 : 190 : M161
		(ii) T65 : T76 : 77 : 73
	EH	(i) P48 : P22 : 507 : 285
		(ii) P19 : 375 : 42 : 286
Anthems	A	58 : 31
	B	73 : 45 : 123
	C	106 : 20

34. The Holy Mountain

Hymns	MHB	(i) 15 : 260 : 276 : 907 : 904
		(ii) 15 : 4 : 276 : 699 : 904
	HP	(i) 50 : 242 : 431 : 531 : 822
		(ii) 56 : 438 : 558 : 629 : 811
Anthems	A	65
	B	4
	C	1 : 38

35. The Incarnation

Hymns	HP	(i) 101 : 102 : 107 : 114 : 666
		(ii) 90 : 92 : 95 : 109 : 126
	AMR	(i) 63 : 432 : 68 : 71
	or	68 M129
		(ii) 69 : 544 : 64 : 67
	or	M194 M120
	EH	(i) 27 : 605 : 19 : P8
		(ii) 20 : 209 : 25 : P21
Anthems	A	19 : 75 : 90
	B	28 : 95 : 96
	C	101 : 20 : 22

36. The King and the Kingdom : Conflict

Hymns	MHB	(i) 426 : 620 : 494 : 736 : 24HS
		(ii) 426 : 822 : 491 : 433 : 70
	HP	(i) 272 : 663 : 672 : 712 : 718
		(ii) 278 : 544 : 688 : 715 : 719
	AMR	(i) 239 : 315 : 324 : 291
	or	M103
		(ii) 102 : 276 : 91 : 303
	EH	(i) P57 : P25 : 302 : 467
		(ii) P27 : 495 om.vv.3, 4 : 72 : 479
Anthems	a	53 : 79
	B	(i) 43
		(ii) 108
	C	91 : 43

37. The King and the Kingdom: Suffering

Hymns	MHB	(i) 26 : 395 : 110 : 144 : 503
		(ii) 907 : 618 : 448 : 729 : 195
	HP	(i) 209 : 528 : 696 : 713 : 817
		(ii) 436 : 562 : 685 : 708 : 711
	AMR	(i) 393 pt 1 : 289 : 333 : 218
	or	M163
		(ii) T87 : 261 : 333 : 356
		(i) 306 : 452 : 484 : 147
		(ii) P28 : 398 : 484 : 505
Anthems	A	24 : 72
	B	(i) 5
		(ii) 76
	C	11 : 25 : 58

38. The King and the Kingdom: Temptation

Hymns	MHB	(i) 92 : 165 : 90HS : 178 : 85HS
		(ii) 427 : 849 : 165 : 626 : 608
	HP	(i) 131 : 264 : 533 : 720 : 790
		(ii) 130 : 235 : 422 : 544 : 667
	AMR	(i) 92 : 204 : 90 : 300
	or	M197
		(ii) M139 : 204 : 90 : 300
	EH	(i) 73 : 90 : P77 : 369
		(ii) 404 : 83 : 86 : 369
Anthems	A	20 : 49
	B	(i) 39
		(ii) 71
	C	29 : 111

39. The King and the Kingdom: Transfiguration

Hymns	MHB	(i) 587 : 183 : 340 : 168 : 550
		(ii) 78 : 526 : 544 : 586 : 85
	HP	(i) 155 : 157 : 158 : 184 : 763
		(ii) 156 : 267 : 269 : 458 : 531
	AMR	(i) 372 : 205 : 318 : 560
		(ii) 249 : 559 : 422 : 561
	or	M169 M200
	EH	(i) 407 : 437 : 235 : P53
		(ii) 637 : P52 : 312 : 236
	or	P53
Anthems	A	65 : 93
	B	(i) 36
		(ii) 64
	C	47 : 4

40. The King and the Kingdom:
The Victory of the Cross

Hymns	MHB	(i) 184 : 854 : 179 : 243 : 40HS
		(ii) 368 : 180 : 177 : 62HS : 176
	HP	(i) 174 : 177 : 182 : 227 : 262
		(ii) 165 : 167 : 170 : 231 : 799
	AMR	(i) 97 vv.1,2,3,5,7,8 : 215 : 395 : 268
		(ii) 96 : 398 : 108 : 107
	or	M164
	EH	(i) 96 : 510 : 333 : 546
		(ii) 94 : 327 : 107 : 99
Anthems	A	86 : 92
	B	110
	C	3 : 68

41. The Lakeside

Hymns	MHB	9HS : 157 : 12HS : 309 : 669
	HP	128 : 141 : 467 : 532 : 673
	AMR	142 : T98 : 137 : 140
	EH	627 : 137 : 127 : 134
Anthems	A	22
	B	78
	C	51

42. The Life of Faith

| Hymns | MHB | (i) 64 : 604 : 694 : 507 : 105 |
| | | (ii) 413 : 588 : 375 : 382 : 390 |

HP	(i) 442 : 451 : 686 : 735 : 767	
	(ii) 662 : 675 : 682 : 683 : 684	
AMR	(i) 404 : 571 : T79 : 330	
or		M128
	(ii) 245 : 196 : T39 : 206	
EH	(i) P64 : 197 : P59 : 344	
	(ii) 422 : 446 : P61 : 406	

Anthems
A	22 : 76
B	(i) 117
	(ii) 101
C	8 : 110

43. The Life of the Baptized

Hymns
MHB	924 : 1HS : 404 : 399 : 721
HP	421 : 513 : 583 : 703 : 773
AMR	374 : 140 vv.1, 3 : 396 : 257
EH	P90 : P23 : 320 : 393

Anthems
A	56
B	24
C	24

44. The Mind of Christ

Hymns
MHB	(i) 420 : 632 : 714 : 557 : 2HS
	(ii) 253 : 5 : 465 : 74HS : 892
HP	(i) 65 : 253 : 291 : 739 : 773
	(ii) 294 : 303 : 318 : 394 : 724
AMR	(i) 189 pt 2 : T4 : 388 : 342
	(ii) 208 : T41 : 195 : T70

	EH	(i) 419 pt 2 : P85 : 418 : 433
		(ii) 408 : 456 : 238 : P59
		(Part 1)

Anthems	A	64 : 74
	B	(i) 73
		(ii) 75
	C	79

45. The More Excellent Way

Hymns	MHB	(i) 659 : 138 : 56HS : 911 : 431
		(ii) 10 : 43 : 18HS : 435 : 44HS
	HP	(i) 40 : 301 : 745 : 757 : 766
		(ii) 36 : 45 : 134 : 216 : 725
	AMR	(i) 380 : 233 : T29 : 329
	or	M132
		(ii) T32 : 232 : 205 : 203
	EH	(i) P88 : 396 : P24 : 343
		(ii) 438 : 453 : 437 : 460

Anthems	A	67 : 85
	B	(i) 129
		(ii) 102
	C	54 : 88

46. The Neighbour

Hymns	MHB	(i) 524 : 97HS : 145 : 55HS : 444
		(ii) 147 : 871 : 884 : 893 : 895
	HP	(i) 147 : 342 : 349 : 394 : 401
		(ii) 281 : 343 : 350 : 431 : 802

AMR	(i)	480 : 262 vv.1–4 : T100 : T97
	(ii)	T82 : 235 : 207 : T48
EH	(i)	521 : 554 vv.1–4 : P98 : 126
	(ii)	P91 : 152 : 529 : P99
A		78 : 25
B	(i)	103
	(ii)	25
C		55 : 84

47. The New Dispensation

Hymns	MHB	(i)	410 : 840 : 561 : 18HS : 17
		(ii)	12 : 822 : 20HS : 22 : 815
	HP	(i)	216 : 279 : 414 : 487 : 742
		(ii)	293 : 423 : 458 : 536 : 684
Anthems	A		21
	B		98
	C		90

48. The New Law

Hymns	MHB	460 : 286 : 306 : 596 : 912
	HP	61 : 289 : 407 : 634 : 723
	AMR	370 : T34 : 235 : T70
	or	M162 M152
	EH	635 : P62 : 152 : P86
Anthems	A	54
	B	22
	C	8 : 55

49. The New Man

Hymns	MHB	(i) 17 : 842B : 371 : 562 : 892
		(ii) 493 : 868 : 898 : 37HS : 431
	HP	(i) 216 : 335 : 699 : 726 : 738
		(ii) 39 : 149 : 500 : 583 : 791
	AMR	(i) 369 : 337 : 364 : T46
		(ii) 326 : T66 : 334 : T46
	or	M146 M156
	EH	(i) 481 : 485 : 316 : P81
		(ii) 445 : P24 : 499 : P87
Anthems	A	58 : 60
	B	(i) 67
		(ii) 86
	C	34 : 67

50. The New Temple

Hymns	MHB	(i) –
		(ii) 702 : 567 : 707 : 430 : 892
	HP	(i) 448 : 653 : 656 : 784 : 808
		(ii) 494 : 510 : 549 : 658 : 724
	AMR	(i) 243 : 260 : 256 : 494
	or	M5131
		(ii) 245 : 632 : 259 : T88
	EH	(i) P57 : P56 : 545 : P77
		(ii) 422 : 535 pt 2 : 464 : 329
Anthems	A	58 : 94
	B	(i) 16 : 65
		(ii) 21 : 65
	C	48 : 52

51. The Offering of Life

Hymns	MHB	(i) 9 : 968 : 741 : 742 : 572
		(ii) 11 : 395 : 345 : 387 : 600
	HP	(i) 215 : 532 : 653 : 743 : 797
		(ii) 391 : 469 : 544 : 623 : 705
	AMR	(i) 3 pt 1 : T48 : 341 : T62
		(ii) 3 pt 2 : 229 : T5 : 329
	EH	(i) 257 pt 1 : 522 : 429 : 582
		(ii) 257 pt 3 : 518 : P102 : 343
Anthems	A	39 : 89
	B	(i) 88
		(ii) 21
	C	45 : 46 : 97 : 114 : 115

52. The People of God

Hymns	MHB	685 : 588 : 576 : 718 : 386
	HP	303 : 433 : 486 : 491 : 513
	AMR	248 : 260 : 254 : T83
	or	M196
	EH	P71 : P58 : 488 : P77
Anthems	A	33
	B	85
	C	50

53. The Presentation in the Temple

Hymns	MHB	113 : 855 : 30HS : 19HS : 88
	HP	80 : 99 : 126 : 446 : 705

Anthems   A   90

           B   90 : 108

           C   116

54. The Promise of Redemption : Moses

Hymns   MHB   (i)   68 : 616 :   55 : 890 : 780
                  (ii)   48 : 242 : 485 : 615 : 260

           HP   (i)   62 : 447 : 535 : 730 : 822
                  (ii)   26 :   39 : 437 : 450 : 566

           AMR   (i) 377 : 298 : 389 : 629
                  (ii) T18 : 571 : 285 : 379

           EH   (i) 532 : P106 : 321 : 643
                  (ii) 461 :   197 : 498 : 533

Anthems   A   50 : 74

           B   (i) 121
                    (ii) 113

           C   2 : 53

55. The Proof of Faith

Hymns   MHB   (i)   70 : 490   : 79HS : 706 : 605
                  (ii)   4 : 842A : 495   : 812 : 405

           HP   (i)   63 :   86 : 318 : 677 : 733
                  (ii)   73 : 325   : 466 : 511 : 544

           AMR   (i) 382 : 327 : 177 : 310
           or   M152
                  (11) 366 : 347 : T56 : 290

           EH   (i) 536 vv.1–3, 7 : P70 : 511 : 537
                  (ii) 478 : 421 : P86 : 502

Anthems   A   3 : 83

           B   (i) 14
                     (ii) 89

           C   26 : 89

56. The Remnant of Israel

Hymns   MHB   (i) 305 : 821 : 578 : 260 : 608
                        (ii) 64 : 619 : 778 : 532 : 252

            HP   (i) 53 : 73 : 429 : 454 : 540
                        (ii) 446 : 447 : 453 : 721 : 781

            AMR   (i) 247 : T24 : 633 : T88
            or   M127
                        (ii) 371 : 362 : 271 : T52

            EH   (i) P72 : 435 : P62 : 329
                        (ii) 517 : 545 vv. 1, 3, 5 : 548 : 556

Anthems   A   30 : 66

           B   (i) 15
                     (ii) 52

           C   14 : 49 : 104

57. The Resurrection and the Life

Hymns   MHB   661 : 83HS : 235 : 231 : 247

            HP   137 : 191 : 196 : 521 : 575

            AMR   603 : 132 : T95 : 137
            or   M122

            EH   P31 : 137   : P36 : 127

Anthems	A	15
	B	41
	C	118

58. The Right Use of the Sabbath

Hymns	MHB	(i) 663 : 8HS : 66HS : 784 : 23
		(ii) 2 : 664 : 373 : 66HS : 313
	HP	(i) 499 : 514 : 548 : 575 : 576
		(ii) 500 : 577 : 648 : 655 : 788
Anthems	A	78
	B	119
	C	119 : 40

59. The Serving Community

Hymns	MHB	(i) 665 : 897 : 401 : 598 : 3HS
		(ii) 270 : 401 : 595 : 36HS : 715
	HP	(i) 758 : 776 : 793 : 798 : 804
		(ii) 375 : 381 : 383 : 626 : 785
AMR		(i) 371 : 506 vv. 1,2,5,6 : 331 : 336
	or	M1
		(ii) 177 : 254 : T34 : 328
	or	M122
EH		(i) 517 : 178, vv.1, 2, 5, 6 : 577 : 259
		(ii) 511 : 488 : 448 : 329
Anthems	A	44 : 55
	B	(i) 62
		(ii) 7
	C	25 : 98

60. The Suffering Community

Hymns	MHB	(i) 253 : 488 : 789 : 727 : 489
		(ii) 90 : 1HS : 492 : 728 : 265
	HP	(i) 556 : 571 : 708 : 711 : 713
		(ii) 65 : 227 : 253 : 696 : 783
	AMR	(i) 181 : 261 : 183 : 267
		(ii) 175 : 182 : 289 : 294
	EH	(i) 394 : 398 : 362 : 551 vv.1 ,3
		(ii) P92 : 385 : 452 : 426
Anthems	A	46 : 92
	B	(i) 56 : 94
		(ii) 94 : 123
	C	52 : 58

61. The Two Ways

Hymns	HP	529 : 701 : 722 : 748
	AMR	408 : 250 : 184 : 259
	EH	P58 : 436 : 383 : 341
Anthems	A	4 : 20
	B	(i) 42
		(ii) 53 : 54
	C	12 : 53

62. The Upper Room Appearances

| Hymns | MHB | 214 : 213 : 235 : 719 : 4HS |
| | HP | 188 : 194 : 199 : 669 : 763 |

	AMR	132 : 603 : 130 : 139
	EH	137 : P31 : 626 : 128
Anthems	A	10
	B	40 : 41
	C	42

63. The Visit to Jerusalem

	MHB	113 : 164 : 266 : 81HS : 163
	HP	1 : 127 : 143 : 282 : 522
Anthems	A	79
	B	73
	C	13

64. The Way of the Cross

Hymns	HMB	(i) 84 : 837 : 12HS : 381 : 192
		(ii) 84 : 92HS : 12HS : 381 : 192
	HP	(i) 159 : 160 : 163 : 166 : 221
		(ii) 159 : 160 : 161 : 162 : 173
	AMR	(Set 1) 98 : 225 vv.1, 3 : 102 : 107
		(Set 2) 597 : 99 : 111 : 108
		or M184
	EH	(Set 1) 622 : 368 vv.1, 3 : P27 : 99
		(Set 2) 622 : 620 : 102 : 107
Anthems	A	16 : 17 : 40
	B	(i) 81
		(ii) 128
	C	16 : 44 : 86 : 87

65. The Way, the Truth, and the Life

Hymns	MHB	930 : 160 : 12HS : 635 : 105
	HP	234 : 254 : 557 : 734 : 735
	AMR	139 : 199 : 279 : 602 vv. 11–13
	EH	128 : P74 : 431 : P37
Anthems	A	39
	B	26
	C	66 : 103 : 106

66. The Wedding at Cana

Hymns	MHB	259 : 35 : 623 : 717 : 107
	HP	142 : 148 : 261 : 273 : 458
Anthems	A	62
	B	75
	C	106

67. The Whole Armour of God

Hymns	MHB	(i) 78 : 484 : 577 : 533 : 98
		(ii) 14 : 484 : 539 : 482 : 670
	HP	(i) 275 : 677 : 710 : 719 : 721
		(ii) 378 : 436 : 688 : 695 : 712
	AMR	(i) 175 : 303 : 294 : 304
		(ii) 183 vv. 1, 2 : 293 : 307 : 291
	EH	(i) P92 : 479 : 449 : 389
		(ii) 362 vv. 1, 2 : 402 : 581 : 467

Anthems   A   9 : 59

            B   (i) 43
                   (ii) 98

            C   1

68. The Wisdom of God

Hymns   HP   9 : 24 : 32 : 76 : 674

          AMR 42 : T10 : T60 : 636

          EH   P68 : P75 : P87 : P67

Anthems   A   51

            B   88

            C   107

69. The Wise Men

Hymns   MHB (i) 122 : 133 : 132 : 137 : 862

                (ii) 142 : 862 : 138 : 137 : 122

          HP   (i) 89 : 107 : 121 : 123 : 128
                (ii) 105 : 109 : 128 : 505 : 714

Anthems   A   23 : 48

            B   (i) 71
                   (ii) 18

            C   7 : 80 : 63

70. The Witnessing Community

Hymns   MHB (i) 424 : 396 : 747 : 36HS : 42HS
                (ii) 93 : 396 : 923 : 73HS : 42HS

| | HP | (i) 269 : 278 : 570 : 770 : 804 |
| | | (ii) 2 : 322 : 774 : 787 : 789 |

	AMR	(i) 264 : T72 : 220 : 417
	or	M177
		(ii) 221 : 219 om. vv.4, 5 : T11 : 305

| | EH | (i) 395 : P105 : 420 : 310 |
| | | (ii) 376 : 45 om. vv.4, 5 : 552 : P94 |

Anthems A 34 : 66

B (i) 48
   (ii) 27

C 81 : 82

71. The Word of God in the Old Testament

Hymns MHB (i) 678 : 848 : 50 : 310 : 303
             (ii) 428 : 308 : 418 : 310 : 359

HP (i) 469 : 479 : 481 : 483 : 523
    (ii) 64 : 82 : 429 : 480 : 663

AMR (i) 252 : T15 : T90 : 48
or   M157
     (ii) 53 : 250 : T54 : 267
or   M134 250

EH (i) 11 : P66 : P83 : 552
    (ii)   6 : 436 : P5 : 551 vv.1, 3

Anthems A 22 : 44

B (i) 130 : 44
   (ii) 11 : 44

72. Those in Authority

Hymns MHB (i) 47HS : 620 : 882 : 25HS : 891
             (ii) 3   : 810 : 3HS : 25HS : 883

	HP	(i)	61 : 227 : 402 : 406 : 414
		(ii)	245 : 404 : 409 : 426 : 546

	AMR	(i)	166 : 583 : T63 : 375
		(ii)	630 : 581 : T99 : 263
	or		M189

	EH	(i)	365 : 562 : P104 : 427
		(ii)	P63 : 561: 563 : 504

Anthems	A	70 : 84
	B	(i) 72
		(ii) 100
	C	74 : 107

73. Work

Hymns	MHB	(i) 929 : 872 : 686 : 908 : 586
		(ii) 927 : 926 : 577 : 87HS : 590
	HP	(i) 342 : 375 : 376 : 380 : 381
		(ii) 377 : 383 : 384 : 619 : 636

Anthems	A	11 : 13
	B	7
	C	84 : 98

74A. Christmas Eve: Midnight Service

Hymns	MHB	(i) 129 : 123 : 76HS : 121 : 125
		(ii) 125 : 129 : 76HS : 121 : 131
	HP	(i) 79 : 91 : 95 : 112 : 113
		(ii) 107 : 108 : 115 : 119 : 120
	AMR	(i) 65 : 58 : 390 : 60
		(ii) 65 : 58 : 390 : 60

	EH	(i) 15 : 613 vv.1, 4, 5, 6 : 318 : 24
		(ii) 15 : 613 vv.1, 4, 5, 6 : 318 : 24
Anthems	A	90 : 91
	B	3 : 106
	C	22

74B. Christmas Day: Morning Service

Hymns	MHB	(i) 129 : 119 : 131 : 118 : 117
		(ii) 120 : 124 : 143 : 117 : 118
	HP	(i) 92 : 103 : 106 : 110 : 120
		(ii) 96 : 104 : 105 : 110 : 117
	AMR	(i) 61 pt 1 : 62 : 593 : 61 pt 2
		(ii) 61 pt 1 : 62 : 593 : 61 pt 2
	EH	(i) 21 : 30 : 614 : P9
		(ii) 21 : 30 : 614 : P9
Anthems	A	75 : 90 : 91
	B	27 : 95 : 96
	C	101 : 20

75. Easter Day

Hymns	MHB	(i) 204 : 70HS : 212 : 216 : 29HS
		(ii) 205 : 208 : 29HS : 216 : 213
	HP	(i) 109 : 193 : 202 : 213 : 214
		(ii) 186 : 191 : 193 : 198 : 208
	AMR	(Set 1) 134 : 422 : T95 : 141
		(Set 2) 134 : 140 : 131 : 141
		(Set 3) 134 : 135 : 133 : 141

EH	(Set 1)	133 : P30 : P36 : 135
	(Set 2)	133 : 134 : P38 : 135
	(Set 3)	133 : 625 : 131 : 135

Anthems	A	1 : 13 : 37
	B	12 : 38 : 60 : 120
	C	9 : 26 : 92 : 119 : 27 : 28

76. Pentecost: Whit Sunday

Hymns	MHB	(i) 273 : 283 : 290 : 730 : 278
		(ii) 293 : 277 : 289 : 290 : 273
	HP	(i) 283 : 305 : 314 : 320 : 324
		(ii) 281 : 285 : 287 : 306 : 313
	AMR	156 : 153 : 155 : T26
	or	M111 M 170
		157 : 615 : 234 : T98
	or	M171 M145
	EH	155 : 631 : P43 : P44
		153 : P44 : 458 : P43

Anthems	A	2 : 18 : 28
	B	(i) 82
		(ii) 2 : 34
	C	(i) 3 : 6 : 112
		(ii) 12 : 60 : 112

77. Trinity Sunday : Pentecost 1

Hymns	MHB	(i) 36 : 279 : 39 : 40 : 573
		(ii) 36 : 37 : 38 : 795 : 49HS
	HP	(i) 7 : 18 : 336 : 445 : 513
		(ii) 4 : 6 : 219 : 695 : 710

AMR	(i&ii)	160 : 159 : 401 : 162 vv.1,2,5,8,9
or		161 164 M187
EH	(i&ii)	162 : 161pt 2 : P45 : 212 vv.1,2,5,8,9
or		372 387

Anthems	A	6 : 71
	B	(i) 82
		(ii) 2
	C	(i) 3 : 6
		(ii) 12 : 60

Festivals and Special Occasions

78. All Saints Day: 1 November

Hymns	MHB	(morning)	(i) 7 : 668 : 745 : 831 : 652B
			(ii) 830 : 616 : 824 : 697 : 831
		(evening)	(i) 25 : 818 : 593 : 590 : 828
			(ii) 26 : 639 : 181 : 498 : 833
	HP	(morning)	(i) 484 : 814 : 815 : 818 : 821
			(ii) 4 : 444 : 722 : 810 : 812
		(evening)	(ii) 15 : 20 : 273 : 358 : 447

AMR		272 : 571 : 527 : 624
	or	371 : 528 : M175 : 531
	or	M199 : M155 : 570 : T30

EH		428 197 641 639
	or	517 199 204 196
	or	519 P55 P54

Anthems	A	77 : 93
	B	(i) 57
		(ii) 50
	C	1 : 35 : 45 : 46 : 78 : 96 : 97

79. Remembrance Sunday

Hymns   MHB   (i) 878 : 237 : 896 : 903 : 832
                           (ii) 878 : 897 : 7HS : 912 : 832

           HP   (i) 203 : 233 : 358 : 412 : 712
                           (ii) 358 : 406 : 426 : 485 : 814

           AMR   165 : T14 : T63 : T34
           or   380   T69   M189   M179

           EH   450 : P33 : 562 : P101
           or   544   P82   P104   P102

Anthems   A   49 : 82

           B   (i) 42
                       (ii) 62

           C   21 : 96

80. Christian Citizenship Sunday: Third Sunday in November

Hymns   MHB   (i) 13   : 34HS : 884 : 898 : 923
                           (ii) 9HS : 894   : 902 : 742 : 891

           HP   (i) 226 : 401 : 403 : 553 : 758
                           (ii) 341 : 389 : 400 : 431 : 456

Anthems   A   44 : 55 : 73

           B   (i) 10
                       (ii) 72

           C   55 : 111

81. Watchnight Service: 31 December

Hymns   MHB   (i) 961 : 17   : 905 : 24HS : 956
                           (ii) 959 : 73HS : 955 : 580   : 956

           HP   (i) 248 : 354 : 358 : 501 : 712
                           (ii) 354 : 356 : 357 : 360 : 440

82. Epiphany or The Manifestation of Christ to the Gentiles: 6 January

Hymns	MHB	(i) 139 : 122 : 135 : 151 : 267
		(ii) 132 : 133 : 9 : 33HS : 256
	HP	(i) 89 : 123 : 124 : 125 : 462
		(ii) 121 : 122 : 239 : 246 : 505
	AMR	79 : 76 : 291 : 220
	or	75 596 M129 260
	EH	39 : 40 : 45 : 420
	or	41 616 P10 P85
Anthems	A	35 : 48
	B	(i) 71
		(ii) 18
	C	70 : 80 : 63

83. Ash Wednesday or The First Day of the Season called Lent

Hymns	MHB	(i) 90 : 180 : 556 : 391 : 490
		(ii) 245 : 183 : 248 : 53HS : 420
	HP	(i) 154 : 178 : 536 : 697 : 710
		(ii) 130 : 167 : 171 : 280 : 744
	AMR	(Set 1) 325 : 324 : 367
		or 304 349
		(Set 2) 326 : T57 : 259 : 236
	EH	(Set 1) 82 : 389 : 316 : 424
		(Set 2) 445 : 442 : 464 : P76
Anthems	A	20 : 43
	B	19 : 86
	C	17 : 30

84. Holy Week

Because of the great diversity of liturgical practice in the Church of England during Holy Week, no Anglican selection can be usefully suggested. As the Introduction has made clear, Anglican lists refer to the eucharist; Maundy Thursday is the only day on which a eucharist with hymns is general in *most* parishes – and on this occasion a selection is hardly difficult.

(a) Monday : Penitence

Hymns   MHB   (i) 173 : 174 : 90HS : 201 : 345
    (ii) 179 : 350 : 349   : 353 : 182

    HP   (i) 185 : 424 : 533 : 539 : 543
    (ii) 134 : 419 : 429 : 529 : 697

(b) Tuesday : Obedience

Hymns   MHB   (i) 784 : 239 : 500 : 236 : 589
    (ii) 452 : 575 : 90 : 406 : 529

    HP   (i) 141 : 235 : 533 : 794 : 807
    (ii) 47 : 247 : 383 : 523 : 527

(c) Wednesday : Service

Hymns   MHB   (i) 48HS : 782 : 178 : 144 : 388
    (ii) 48HS : 581 : 144 : 579 : 521

    HP   (i) 169 : 174 : 560 : 745 : 796
    (ii) 172 : 173 : 216 : 248 : 375

(d) Maundy Thursday : The Upper Room

Hymns   MHB   (i) 763 : 84HS : 771 : 770 : 628
    (ii) 763 : 84HS : 760 : 35HS : 181

    HP   (i) 600 : 613 : 615 : 624 : 629
    (ii) 541 : 550 : 593 : 612 : 614

Anthems   A   14 : 16 : 17

         B   (i) 126
             (ii) 59

         C   37

(e) Good Friday : The Death of Christ

Hymns   MHB   (i) 189 : 183 : 93HS : 186 : 182
                  (ii) 191 : 183 : 193   : 200 : 197

           HP   (i) 166 : 167 : 175 : 180 : 181
                  (ii) 165 : 179 : 184 : 273 : 550

Anthems   A   72 : 73 : 82

         B   (i) 91
             (ii) 13

         C   3 : 68

(f) Saturday: Easter Vigil and Communion

Hymns   MHB   (i) 723 : 53HS : 190 : 768 : 731/209
                  (ii) 184 : 94   : 556 : 770 : 773/209

           HP   (i) 172 : 554 : 593 : 620 : 625
                  (ii) 179 : 599 : 600 : 613 : 629

Anthems   A   10

         B   111

         C   83

85. Ascension Day: The Ascension of Christ

Hymns   MHB   (i) 219 : 225 : 221 : 230 : 231
                  (ii) 221 : 224 : 219 : 227 : 228

	HP	(i) 22 : 189 : 197 : 207 : 209
		(ii) 194 : 206 : 222 : 253 : 512
	AMR	610 vv.1–4 : 439 : 224 : 421
	EH	143 : 144 : 481 : 147
Anthems	A	27 : 81
	B	63 : 87
	C	5 : 15

86. Aldersgate Sunday: 24 May or the preceding Sunday

Hymns	MHB	(i) 78 : 842B : 361 : 1 : 375
		(ii) 426 : 5 : 371 : 311 : 386
	HP	(i) 8 : 433 : 684 : 706 : 744
		(ii) 216 : 278 : 703 : 745 : 805
Anthems	A	57 : 66
	B	51 : 118
	C	109 : 81

87. Harvest Thanksgiving

Hymns	MHB	(i) 962 : 18 : 907 : 599 : 963
		(ii) 963 : 969 : 971 : 55HS : 964
	HP	(i) 27 : 342 : 350 : 352 : 355
		(ii) 337 : 348 : 349 : 352 : 603
	AMR	482 : 338 : M167 : T82
	or	484 : 485 : M124 : 267
	EH	289 : 290 : 293 : P59
	or	292 P99

Anthems   A   38 : 42 : 57 : 68

            B   83 : 92

            C   57 : 105 : 93

88. Education Sunday: Ninth Sunday before Easter

Hymns   MHB   (i)   48 : 164 : 56HS : 55   : 32
                     (ii) 929 : 872 : 302   : 67HS : 42HS

          HP   (i)   26 :   39 : 143 : 377 : 803
                  (ii)   76 : 378 : 380 : 560 : 737

An Anglican selection may be found under the Ninth Sunday before Easter: Christ the Teacher

Anthems   A   3 : 79

            B   74 : 109

            C   79 : 91

89. Overseas Missions

Hymns   MHB   (i)   75 : 798 : 703 : 810 : 815
                     (ii) 802 : 817 : 803 : 789 : 809

          HP   (i) 237 : 520 : 769 : 774 : 789
                  (ii)   29 : 238 : 343 : 481 : 804

An Anglican selection may be found under the Twelfth Sunday after Pentecost: The Witnessing Community

Anthems   A   55 : 63

            B   46 : 48

            C   75 : 100

90. Church Anniversary or Festival of Dedication

| Hymns | MHB | (i) 683 : 676 : 680 : 715 : 702 |
| | | (ii) 678 : 701 : 91 : 979 : 706 |

| | HP | (i) 435 : 442 : 531 : 653 : 659 |
| | | (ii) 485 : 515 : 658 : 660 : 817 |

| | AMR | P112 : 260 : 245 : T52 : 476 |
| | or | 620 vv.5–9 248 |

| | EH | 170 : P57 : P56 : 556 |
| | or | 422 |

Anthems	A	39 : 61 : 63
	B	45 : 49
	C	10 : 12 : 50 : 73

91. Mid Lent: Alternative to Lent IV

Anthems	A	44 : 83
	B	33 : 114
	C	94

Abbreviations for Anthems

Publishers

B	Banks of York
BH	Boosey and Hawkes
Ch	Chappells
N	Novello
OUP	Oxford University Press
R	Roberton
RSCM	The Royal School of Church Music
*	Separate sheet publication
WS	The Williams School of Church Music: Bourne Series

Collections

AC1	Anthems for Choirs: Book 1	OUP
AC4	Anthems for Choirs: Book 4	OUP
CAB	Church Anthem Book	OUP
ITBH	In the Beauty of Holiness	N
IHCP	Into his Courts with Praise	N
IWLP	In Wonder, Love and Praise	N
KOG	King of Glory	N
NAB	The Novello Anthem Book	N
OEAB	The Oxford Easy Anthem Book	OUP
OTAB	The Oxford Tudor Anthem Book	OUP
RT	Rejoice Today	N
SAB	The Sixteenth Century Anthem Book	OUP
SEA	Seven Anthems by Elgar	N
SHT	Sixteen Hymns of Today (for use as simple anthems)	RSCM
STTL	Sing to the Lord	N
STPA	Six Three-Part Anthems	RSCM
TEA	Twelve Easy Anthems	RSCM
WJV	With a Joyful Voice	N

Anthems   A

All anthems are SATB unless otherwise indicated

1.	A Carol for Eastertide	U / SATB
2.	A Carol for Whitsuntide	
3.	A Prayer Canticle	U
4.	A Prayer of St Richard	SS
5.	A Song of Mary	
6.	Above him stood the seraphim	SS
7.	Adam and Christ	
8.	Advent Song	
9.	All from the sun's uprise	
10.	Alleluyas of St James	2 pt
11.	Almighty God	
12.	An Awakening	
13.	An Easter Introit	
14.	An Upper Room	U
15.	Anthem for Spring	SAB
16.	*Ave Verum*	
17.	*Ave Verum*	
18.	Awaken us, Lord, and hasten	
19.	Be peace on earth	SS
20.	Be thou my guardian	U / SATB
21.	Blessed are the pure in heart	
22.	Break Thou the Bread of Life	
23.	Brightest and Best	SAB
24.	Carol of Atonement	U
25.	Cast thy burden	
26.	Choral Hymn for Ascension and/or Advent	
27.	Christ above all glory seated	U
28.	Come Holy Ghost	
29.	Come, thou long expected Jesus	
30.	Comfort, O Lord, the soul	
31.	Doubt not thy Father's care	SS
32.	Fairest Lord Jesus	SAB
33.	Fellowship in the Holy Spirit	U / SATB
34.	From all that dwell	

		Subject
Wilson	SHT	75
Routley	SHT	76
Routley	SHT	2 : 55 : 88
White	OEAB	28 : 61
Duffy/Wilson	SHT	12
Dering	OEAB	77
Clarke/Wilson	SHT	25
Holst/Wilson	SHT	11
Tomblings	OEAB	67
arr. Greenings	TEA	62 : 84(f)
Ford	AC1	73
Robson	STTL	21 : 22
Beechey	*B	73 : 75
arr. Wilson	SHT	84(d)
Petri	STPA	57
Elgar	KOG	64 : 84(d)
Mozart	OEAB	64 : 84(d)
Bach	AC1	14 : 76
Crotch/Ley	OEAB	35
Smith/Ley	IWLP	38 : 61 : 83
W. Davies	CAB	12 : 47
J. Watson	IWLP	15 : 41 : 42 : 71
Thrupp/Pasfield	ITBH	69
arr. Greening	TEA	37
Mendelssohn	CAB	4 : 46
arr. Ley	OEAB	11 : 13
Shell	RT	13 : 85
Attwood	CAB	28 : 76
Ley	OEAB	27
Crotch	CAB	1 : 56 : 78
Elgar	SEA	1 : 26 : 30 : 33
Silesian/How	TEA	75
Holst/Wilson	SHT	52
Walmisley	CAB	70

35. From the rising of the sun
36. Give land unto the Lord
37. Glorious the day   SS
38. God, Creator and Lawgiver
39. God is our hope and strength
40. God so loved the world
41. Hail, true body   2 pt
42. Harvest Thanksgiving
43. Hide not thou Thy face
44. Ho, everyone that thirsteth
45. How goodly are the tents
46. Into this world of sorrow
47. Jesu, joy of man's desiring
48. Kings in Glory
49. Lead kindly Light   U / SATB
50. Lead me, Lord
51. Lord, I trust thee
52. Most glorious Lord of life   SAB
53. My eyes for beauty pine   U / SATB
54. New songs of celebration render
55. Now join we to praise the Creator
56. O Christ, O blessed Lord
57. O give thanks   SAB
58. O holy spirit, Lord of grace
59. O Lord God   SSA
60. O most merciful
61. O praise God
62. O sing unto the Lord   S / ATB
63. O Thou who at Thy Eucharist
64. O Word incarnate   SAB
65. O worship the Lord
66. O ye who bear Christ's holy name   2 pt
67. Pastures   SA(T)B
68. Pleasure it is   2 pt
69. Praise
70. Praise the Lord   U
71. Rejoicing in the Trintiy
72. Richard de Castre's Prayer
73. See, Christ was wounded for our sake

Ouseley	CAB	82
arr. Bullock	OEAB	5 : 7
Hill	TEA	75
arr. Palmer	SHT	22 : 26 : 87
Bach	AC1	51 : 65 : 90
Goss	CAB	64
arr. Greening	TEA	15
Rapley	IHCP	87
Tarrant	CAB	84
Benion	IHCP	59 : 71 : 80 : 91
Ouseley	AC1	31
Buck	CAB	27 : 60
Bach	CAB	19
M. Shaw	OEAB	69 : 80
Harris/Gritton	RT	17 : 23 : 38 : 79
Wesley	TEA/AC1	54
Handel	AC1	4 : 18 : 68
Harris	OEAB	7
Howells	OEAB	31 : 36
arr. Wilson	SHT	14 : 48
Laycock	SHT	59 : 80 : 89
Wagner	AC1	43
J. Wood	WJV	86 : 87
Tye	*RSCM	33 : 49 : 50
Buck	CAB	3 : 67
arr. Greening	TEA	49
Gibbs	OEAB	90
Morley	STPA	20 : 66
Woldlike	OEAB	89
Gibbons	6TPA	44
J. Woods	ITBH	6 : 34 : 39
Sampson	NAB	56 : 70 : 86
Ley	IHCP	16 : 45
Cope	OEAB	32 : 87
Rowley	*OUP	10
Greene	TEA	72
Wilson	SHT	77 : 78
Terry	OEAB	37 : 84(e)
Dawney	SHT	80 : 84(e)

74. Shepherd Boy's Song
75. Shepherds Loud
76. Simple Gifts
77. Sing Alleluia forth
78. Sweet is the work   U / SATB
79. Teach me, O Lord
80. Teach me thy way
81. The Lord ascendeth
82. The Lord is risen   SAB
83. The Lord my pasture shall prepare
84. The Mocking of Christ
85. Thee, we adore
86. These are they which follow the Lamb
87. Thou knowest, Lord
88. Turn thy face
89. View me, Lord
90. Virgin-born, we bow before Thee   U
91. Voice of angels
92. *Vox ultima Crucio*   U
93. Ye servants of God
94. Ye servants of the all-bounteous Lord

Alden	SHT	17 : 44 : 54
arr. Rowley	OEAB	35 : 74B
arr. Llewellyn	SHT	29 : 42
Thiman	NAB	5
Robson	NAB	46 : 58
Attwood	AC1	36 : 63 : 88
Fox	WJV	3 : 6
Scheidt/Ley	NAB	85
Morley	STPA	24 : 79
Harris	NAB	23 : 32 : 55 : 91
Tallis/Wilson	SHT	72 : 84 (e)
arr. Greening	TEA	45
Goss	AC1	40
Purcell	CAB	25
Attwood	TEA	9
Lloyd	*N	2 : 51
arr. Greening	TEA	35 : 53 : 74A : 74B
Cameron	WJV	74A : 74B
Harris	OEAB	40 : 60
arr. Coleman	OEAB	39 : 90
Webbe	TEA	8 : 50

B

1. A Hymn of Trust
2. A Hymn to the Trinity
3. A Sound of Angels
4. Above all praise and all majesty
5. Ah, thou poor world
6. All thy works praise thee
7. All who love and serve the city
8. Almighty and everlasting God
9. Almighty Father, who didst give. . .
10. Almighty God, fountain of all wisdom
11. And the glory of the Lord
12. Arise in us
13. As Jesus went to Calvary
14. Awake my soul and with the sun
15. Be still my soul
16. Blest are the pure in heart
17. Bread of the world
18. Brightest and best of the sons
19. Call to remembrance, O Lord
20. *Cantate Domino*
21. Christ from whom all blessings flow
22. Christ is the World's Light
23. Christ, of all my hopes the ground
24. Come down, O love divine
25. Come, Holy Ghost
26. Come, my way, my truth . . .
27. Come ye faithful
28. Come ye gentles
29. Dear Lord and Father of Mankind
30. Dearest Lord Jesus
31. Doubt not thy Father's care
32. Father, we praise thee. . .
33. Flocks in pastures
34. Fountain of sweets
35. Go forth with God
36. God is a spirit

Shave	RT	23
Tchaikovsky	*N	76
Tye	AC1	74A
Mendelssohn	OEAB	34
Brahms	AC1	37
Lloyd Webber	IWLP	22
Thiman	*N	59 : 73
Gibbons	CAB	1 : 30
Westbrook	IWLP	25
Farrar	AC1	80
Handel	*B	27 : 71
M. Shaw	ITBH	75
D. Ratcliffe	STTL	84(e)
Chambers	NAB	55
Lloyd Webber	RT	56
Thiman	NAB	8 : 50
Harker	STTL	16
Thiman	*N	69 : 82
Farrant	CAB	83
Pitoni	AC1	5
Westbrook	RT	8 : 50 : 51
arr. Westbrook	*WS	28 : 48
Handel/Chambers	RT	38 : 43
Harris	IHCP	17 : 29
Thiman	WJV	31 : 46
Harris	KOG	65
Thatcher	OEAB	70
Bairstow	NAB	35 : 74B
Parry/Chambers	NAB	25
Bach	OEAB	11
Elgar/Chambers	IWLP	1
Thiman	NAB	26
Bach/Roper	OEAB	91
Kitson	ITBH	15 : 76
M. Shaw	*OUP	23
Sterndale-Bennett	CAB	39

37. God is gone up on high
38. God is living
39. God of pity, God of grace
40. Good Christian men. . .
41. Good Christian men. . .
42. Had we but hearkened
43. He that shall endure to the end
44. He watching over Israel
45. Here beauty dwells. . .
46. How beauteous are their feet
47. How beautiful upon the mountains
48. How lovely are the messengers
49. How lovely are thy dwellings fair
50. I heard a voice
51. I sing of a maiden
52. If thou shalt confess
53. If ye love me
54. If ye love me
55. Immortal love
56. In heavenly love abiding
57. In the heavenly kingdom
58. In thee is gladness
59. *Jesu, dulcis memoria*
60. Jesu, fount of consolation
61. Jesus the First and Last
62. Judge eternal
63. King all glorious
64. King of glory, King of peace
65. Let all mortal flesh keep silence
66. Let all the world
67. Lift up your hearts
68. Light of the World
69. Light's glittering morn
70. Lo star-led chiefs
71. Lord, for thy tender mercies' sake
72. Lord, make us instruments of thy peace
73. Lord that descendest, Holy Child
74. Lord, thou hast told us
75. Love divine, all loves excelling

arr. H. Walmesley	*B	13
Bach	AC1	75
Westbrook	ITBH	38
Bullock	OEAB	62
Thiman	NAB	62
Davies/Chambers	*N	62 : 79
Mendelssohn	NAB	36 : 67
Mendelssohn	*B	71
Thiman	NAB	33 : 90
Stanford	*N	11 : 89
Stainer	*N	20 : 28
Mendelssohn	*B	70 : 89
Brahms	*N	5 : 90
Goss	CAB	78
Rowley	OEAB	12
Stanford	IWLP	18 : 65 : 86
Heeley	IWLP	61
Tallis	CAB	61
A. F. Barnes	NAB	3
Pritchard	NAB	60
Harris	NAB	78
arr. Stanford	*RSCM	19
Vittoria	*OUP	84(d)
Bach/Sampson	ITBH	75
Barnby / Westbrook	NAB	2
Marchant	NAB	40 : 79
Kitson	IWLP	110 : 85
Thiman	*N	39 : 59
Cashmore	ITBH	8 : 27 : 50
Dyson	N	5 : 1
Chambers	RT	49
Elgar	SEA	20
Wadely	NAB	24 : 38
Crotch	CAB	69 : 82
Hilton/Farrant	OEAB	63 : 72
M. Shaw	STTL	80
Gritton	AC1	33 : 44
Bax	AC4	17 : 88
Lloyd Webber	IWLP	10 : 44 : 66

76. Man that is born of a woman
77. May the grace of Christ our Saviour
78. Most glorious Lord of life
79. My joy, my life, my crown
80. My soul truly waiteth
81. *Nolo mortem peccatoris*
82. O be joyful
83. O Christ, who holds the open gate
84. O clap your hands
85. O come ye servants
86. O for a closer walk
87. O God, the King of Glory
88. O Lord, increase my faith
89. O Love of whom
90. *O nata lux*
91. O Saviour of the World
92. O sing unto the Lord
93. O sweet Jesu
94. O Thou the Central Orb
95. Of the Father's love begotten
96. On this day. . .
97. Praise Him, praise the great Creator
98. Praise to God in the Highest
99. Praise to Thee, Lord Jesus
100. Pray that Jerusalem may have
101. Psalm 150
102. Purest and Highest
103. Rejoice in the Lord always
104. Rejoice today with one accord
105. Saviour, whilst my heart is tender
106. Song 46
107. Songs of praise the angels sang
108. Surely the Lord is in this place
109. Teach me, O Lord, the perfect way
110. The Cross
111. The day draws on
112. The eyes of all wait upon Thee
113. The God of love my shepherd is
114. The Lord is my shepherd

Wesley	CAB	37
Brockless	WJV	21
Gibbs	CAB	41
Montgomery	*OUP	31
J. Wood	RT	12
Morley	SAB	64
C. Wood	IHCP	26 : 76
M. Shaw	KOG	3 : 87
M. Shaw	WJV	13
Tye	AC1	52
arr. Stanford	AC1	49 : 83
Purcell	AC1	85
Gibbons / Loosemore	CAB	4 : 51 : 68
Videro	OEAB	55
Tallis	OTAB	53
Goss	CAB	84(e)
Harris	RT	87
Graves	NAB	6
C. Wood	AC4	11 : 60
Thiman	NAB	35 : 74B
Stewart	AC4	35 : 74B
Bach	ITBH	22
arr. Campbell	AC1	47 : 67
Schütz/Harris	NAB	40
arr. Stanford	*RSCM	72
C. Franck	*N	42
arr. Stanford	*RSCM	45
Anon: sixteenth century	SAB	46
Meale	RT	7
Lloyd Webber	ITBH	14
Gibbons/Jackson	AC1	74A
Thiman	IWLP	6 : 22
Burnell	NAB	36 : 53
Lloyd Webber	RT	88
A. F. Barnes	NAB	40
Bairstow	CAB	84(f)
Harris	*OUP	4 : 10
Wesley/Eades	WJV	4 : 10
Lloyd Webber	IHCP	54

Smart/Passmore	ITBH	32
Thalben-Ball	RT	11
Thiman	IHCP	42
N. Barnes	*B	86
Anon: sixteenth century	SAB	58
arr. Harris	*N	75
Walker Robson	IHCP	16 : 54
Berlioz	*N	33
Jacob	NAB	60
arr. Holst	AC4	9
Bach	AC1	7
Tallis	AC1	84(d)
Wesley	CAB	2
arr. Westbrook	IHCP	64
Rowley	IHCP	14 : 45
Bach/Sampson	NAB	27 : 71

C

1. And I saw a new heaven
2. And I saw another angel
3. As Moses lifted up the serpent
4. As pants the hart
5. *Ascendit Deus*
6. Ascribe unto the Lord
7. Ascribe unto the Lord
8. *Beati quorum via*
9. Blessed be the God and Father
10. Blessed City, heavenly Salem
11. Cast me not away. . .
12. Christ is our corner-stone
13. Christ whose glory fills the skies
14. *Civitas Sancti Tui*
15. *Coelos ascendit hodie*
16. *Drop, drop slow tears*
17. *Expectans, Expectavi*
18. Faire is the heaven
19. For I went with the multitude
20. For unto us a child is born
21. Give us the wings of faith
22. Glory to God
23. God is gone up
24. Grant us Thy peace
25. Greater Love
26. *Haec Dies*
27. Hallelujah Chorus
28. Hallelujah Chorus
29. Hear my prayer
30. Hear my prayer, O Lord
31. Hear the voice and prayer
32. Hosanna to the Son of David
33. Hosanna to the Son of David
34. I am thine, O save me
35. I heard a voice
36. I know that my redeemer lives

Bainton	*N	34 : 67 : 78
Stanford	RT	54
Bairstow	*B	40 : 76 : 77 : 84(e)
Spohr	*N	39
Philips	OTAB	13 : 85
Travers	*N	76 : 77
Wesley	*N	37
M. Shaw	IHCP	61 : 76 : 77 : 90
Armstrong	CAB	55 : 63
Bairstow	*B	90
Wesley	*N	37
M. Shaw		61 : 76 : 77 : 90
Armstrong	CAB	55 : 63
Byrd	*OUP	56
Stanford	*BH	13 : 85
Leighton	*N	64
C. Wood	*Ch	12 : 83
Harris	AC4	5
Aston	*N	26 : 58
Handel	*B	33 : 35 : 74B
Bullock	AC4	79
Handel	*B	35 : 74A
Croft	*N	13
Mendelssohn	CAB	2 : 43
Ireland	AC4	16 : 37 : 59
Byrd	OTAB	75
Beethoven	*B	5 : 75
Handel	*N	75
Mendelssohn	*B	38
Purcell	*N	83
Tallis	OTAB	9
Gibbons	OTAB	11 : 12
Weelkes	OTAB	11 : 12
Wesley	*N	25 : 49
Tomkins	OTAB	78
J. M. Bach	CAB	24

37. I sat down under
38. I saw the Lord
39. I waited for the Lord
40. I was glad
41. I will not leave you comfortless
     (*Non vos relinquam*)
42. If we believe
43. *Insanae et vanae curae*
44. Jesu, grant me this I pray
45. *Justorum Animae*
46. *Justorum Animae*
47. King of glory, King of peace
48. Let all mortal flesh
49. Like as a hart
50. Lo, God is here
51. Lord and master, born to save us
52. Lord it belongs not to my care
53. Lord, thou hast been our refuge
54. Love is a mystery
55. Love is his name
56. Make a joyful noise
57. Maker of man
58. My God and King
59. My soul there is a country
60. O be joyful
61. O be joyful
62. O clap your hands
63. O come let us worship
64. O God, my heart is ready
65. O God, my King
66. O God, thou art my God
67. O hearken Thou
68. O King of the Friday
69. O Lord, give thy Holy Spirit
70. O Lord, in thee do I put my trust
71. O Lord, look down from heaven
72. O pray for the peace of Jerusalem
73. O pray for the peace of Jerusalem
74. O pray for the peace of Jerusalem

Bairstow	AC1	84(d)
Stainer	*N	34
Mendelssohn	*B	69 : 82
Parry	*N	58
Byrd	*N	13 : 17 : 23
Goss	CAB	62
Haydn	*N	36
Gibbons/Bairstow	*B	64
Byrd	OTAB	51 : 78
Stanford	*BH	51 : 78
Davies	KOG	39
Bairstow	AC4	8 : 27 : 50 : 60 : 71
Howells	AC4	56
Grieg/Coleman	IWLP	52 : 90
Franck/Ellis	IWLP	3 : 41
Davies/Wilson	STTL	50
Joubert	*N4	54 : 61
Franck/Ellis	ITBH	28 : 45
Westbrook	*R	10 : 46 : 48 : 80
Mathias	AC4	18
Tunnard	*B	22 : 87
Nelson	*B	37 : 60
Parry	CAB	7
Britten	AC4	26 : 76 : 77
Thalben-Ball	KOG	26
Gibbons	OTAB	13
Mendelssohn	*B	69 : 82
J. Wood	IWLP	19
Amner	AC1	29
Purcell	AC1	30 : 65
Elgar	SEA	49
Nelson	*B	40 : 84(e)
Tallis	OTAB	14
Milner	IHCP	4 : 82
Battishill	*N	25
Blow	*N	21
Taylor	IHCP	7 : 90
Tomkins	SAB	72

Purcell	*N	19 : 89
Vaughan Williams	OEAB	1 : 30
C. Wood	IHCP	4 : 15
Harris	CAB	5 : 78
Boyce	*N	44 : 88
Handel	*N	69 : 82
Wesley	*B	70 : 86
Statham	KOG	70
Rutter	AC1	84(f)
Purcell	*N	46 : 73
Purcell	*N	1
Ashfield	*B	64
Blow	*H	64
Walton	AC4	45
Campbell	*N	55
Barnby	*B	47
Byrd	OTAB	9 : 36 : 88
Middleton	*B	75
Haydn	*B	22 : 87
Schubert/Stainer	*N	91
Stanford	KOG	32
Nares/Bairstow	*B	78/79
Noble	ITBH	51 : 78
Aston	*N	59 : 73
Goss	*B	3 : 20
Wesley	*B	89
Byrd	OTAB	35 : 74B
Gibbons	OTAB	27 : 71
Brydson	ITBH	65
Wesley	CAB	56
Greene	CAB	87
Head	*B	10 : 65 : 66
Wesley	CAB	23 : 68 : 72
Bairstow	*OUP	31
Purcell	*N	86
Rachmaninoff	AC1	42
Boyce	CAB	6 : 38 : 80
Stewart	*N	76
McKie	AC4	11 : 13

Tomkins	OTAB	51
Weelkes	OTAB	51
Eccard	CAB	33 : 53
Schubert	IWLP	5
Handel	*B	57
Stanford	AC1	75